KALI, IN CONVERSATION

A Collection of 30 Prose Poems

KALI, IN CONVERSATION

A Collection of 30 Prose Poems

MAHI RAMAKRISHNAN

ZORBA BOOKS

ZORBA BOOKS

Published by Zorba Books, February 2026
Website: www.zorbabooks.com
Email: info@zorbabooks.com

Title: **Kali, in Conversation**
Author Name: Mahi Ramakrishnan

Softcover ISBN :- 978-93-5896-179-9
Ebook ISBN :- 978-93-5896-303-8

Zorba Books Pvt. Ltd. (opc)
Sushant Arcade,
Next to Courtyard Marriot,
Sushant Lok 1, Gurgaon – 122009, India

Printed in India

REVIEW 1

Mahi's words are an arrow in the eye of The Patriarchy, shattering the cornea of convention and leaving us to contend with our passive blindness. Blindness to the rampant, unquestioning devastation of women from the beginning of time that loudly persists in its ugly pervasiveness. Mahi subtly yet insistently prompts the asking of the uncomfortable. Even in the most tender of moments, her words probe deeply into the reader's psyche.

Kali is a juxtaposition to the reader, emerging as the conscience, the confidante, the other, the mother, the all-encompassing, the soul, the living spirit, the life-giving and the body through which we feel Mahi's poignant pleas. The imagery of Kali that Mahi evokes aesthetically, linguistically and spiritually speaks of a salvation that the reader will find a longing to anchor to.

Every passage feels personal and at the precise moment when the inevitable emotional crash is poised to occur, Mahi resets with a fearless empowerment without betraying the protagonist's anger. Her work justly calls for reading, re-reading, reflection and more reflection without arrogance. Popular myths would have you believe in a Kali superiority and therefore, elusiveness. Mahi masterfully debunks a perceived high-handedness of the Goddess and situates her as every female spirit.

Mahi's work should be required reading as a study on Feminist Literature in The Global Majority.

Gayathri Santhi-McBain

REVIEW 2

Mahi Ramakrishnan is surely Malaysia's most overlooked poet writing in English, quite possibly the best of those living here.

Ramakrishnan's images come at us with that same primal Kali energy of which her subject is formed: a child is "a comet made of giggles and mischief" and a Kali rupa or statue has "eyes like eclipses" (The Child Who Saw Her). It all affirms there's no other way for a poet to write about the goddess Kali than to do so from that entity's liminal territory.

Like Kali, Ramakrishnan's poetry faces all ways at once. She does so fearlessly, without boundaries at times, which makes this collection not one for the faint-hearted, for delicate dispositions or assumed ones. Those averse to nuance or challenge might baulk at some consciously constructed swearing, as well as lines such as

"There is no good or bad," she says
"Only experiences."

This poet is masterful at describing liminal spaces:

We sat together on the floor of the dream
no temple, no body, no rules
Just the two of us
and the weight of everything unsaid.

We didn't speak of grief
but I could feel her hand on the part of me
that still carried my mother's death like a stone

What comes through a thousand times here is a naturalistic, no-holds-barred relationship to the goddess, which screams lived spirituality before anyone can contrive religion into its echo. To contemplate the goddess being one's lover is religiosity's opposite, inevitably recalling, for me, the most striking aspects of 60s and 70s counter-culture: a total, fearless openness to experience.

The world in thrall to so-called social media needs this direct, unmediated and honest experience of spiritual life now more than ever before. Any parent lamenting the dearth of honest and compassionate tales to tell their kids — in the religious sphere especially, right up to contemporary post-truth politics, or what passes for both — Mahi Ramakrishnan's tales offer much remedial warmth.

Lawrence Pettener

REVIEW 3

Conversations with Kali by Mahi Ramakrishna is a mesmerizing collection of 30 poems and prose pieces that boldly turns personal wreckage into a source of terrifying, potent grace.

This collection is not a book, it's a body. It breathes, bleeds, remembers. Its thirty pieces move like incarnations of the same goddess, fractured and reassembled across childhood, desire, violence, lineage, survival. Kali doesn't arrive here in temples or scriptures; she appears in kitchens, hospital rooms, bedrooms, circus tents, small alleys where little girls are sold, and in the quiet corner of a son's dream. The writing doesn't worship her. It wrestles with her, touches her mouth, calls her in moments of exhaustion, daring, grief. She is the pulse beneath every wound the world tries to hide.

The work bends myth until it confesses what patriarchy has always erased. It spits out sanitized epics and replaces them with the messy truth of women who burn and rise. Mothers, daughters, lovers, defiant survivors who do not ask permission to exist. The text never begs to be 'beautiful'. It is stubbornly alive. Tender when it wants to be, brutal when it must. Every piece is a remembering: of bodies that were taught to shrink, of girls who were traded, of women who learned to roar in silence until the silence broke. Somewhere between the shattered altar and the single hibiscus, you feel it…...this is not mythology. It is lineage.

This is the book you read when you are ready to meet the deepest, most powerful version of yourself.

Kanaa Pillai

REVIEW 4

What does it mean to have a personal relationship with the Goddess Kali? It's not an easy relationship - Kali is complex, dark, demanding, mysterious in her intent and unflinching in her opinions- but then again, so is Mahi Ramakrishnan.

Though this series of poems, Mahi explores personhood, personal growth, the boundaries of her relationships, justice and retribution and inherent snobbery. Mahi's approach borders on the irreverent at times. Her Kali is not content to sit on a pedestal, she is far more likely to pick up said pedestal and cosh you over the head with it. This Kali goes into the marginal spaces. She watches over the child who is sold by her father for profit, she lends power to women in conflict zones, she appears to children and fools.

Mahi's relationship with the goddess is conflicted, as most good relationships are. We can love, laugh, hate, lust and resent in equal measure. Frustrations lead the way to self-awareness. This is life. Mahi writes with maturity, with deft use of language and nuance to express her feeling, because these poems are threaded with raw emotions. It would be all too easy for a work of this kind to descend into self-indulgence and even sentimentality but Mahi keeps it well in check. The result is a tightly woven narrative of a relationship between a girl and her goddess. Inspiring, interesting and not to be taken lightly.

Sheena Gurbakhash

CONTENTS

FOREWORD

This is an extraordinary 'book'.

Extraordinary is the best single word I can come up with – but it is woefully inadequate.

I'm not even entirely sure this is a 'book' in any conventional sense.

It's more like a Pandora's Box … when you open the lid, you are swept back by an overwhelming tsunami powered by **thousands of years** of *rage against oppression,* of *righteousness against injustice*, of *courage against cowardice*, of *compassion against inhumanity*. It's a wave of consciousness that you should not resist … just surrender into its flow.

***

So much wisdom is stitched throughout this tapestry that it seems subtle and understated.

There is *profound* wisdom …

'You don't have to fix it all,' she said. 'You just have to be here. … You're not here to be useful. You're here to be alive.'

There is *everyday* wisdom …

'And when you give, make sure the person receiving does not feel humiliated.'

This wisdom is imparted so generously, so graciously, and so casually … it doesn't preach, it just is.

***

If this book had been published by a more conventional publisher with a more traditional Editor, they would have insisted that the content be more *structured.* But this content is Flow! You can't structure Flow … you just let it *flow* …

It takes an hour or two to read this book – I strongly recommend that you do this in one sitting. Put yourself in a quiet place where you will not be disturbed, turn off your phone and any possible distraction, and plunge into this 'book' and don't look back – like jumping into a whirlpool of swirling water that will wash away any illusion of control that you have. *Do not presume! Do not judge!* Just surrender into this torrent and let its raging force carry you … and if you've ever been a heartless and impervious participant in Man's inhumanity to Woman … perhaps be *afraid.*

She observes, she doesn't forget, she empowers, she levels the battlefield … and she laughs …

Imran Ahmad

ACKNOWLEDGEMENTS

This book was born in the shadows and the light, carried by many hands, anchored by many spirits. I could not have walked this path alone, and these pages are an offering to all who shaped the voice that rises here, fierce and tender, like Goddess Kali herself.

To my Amma, Gowrie, who moved through the world with a quiet, unshakeable strength. She taught me that endurance does not mean silence, and that a woman's power is often forged in the spaces where others expect her to break. Every poem that seeks the fire in a woman's belly carries her imprint. Thank you for showing me what courage looks like everyday.

To my Appa, Ramakrishnan, who cultivated values without indoctrination and allowed me space to question, doubt, as well as rebuild myself over and over. He gave me the gift of freedom: to think, to explore, to resist the easy truths. Because of him, I learned that self-discovery is not rebellion; it is birth right. I hold that lesson close.

To Charles, my mentor and compass: you believed in my voice in the seasons when all I could hear inside myself was static. You held space for my uncertainty, my rage, my searching and insisted that there was something worth tending there. This book exists because you refused to let me disappear into doubt. I carry deep gratitude for your guidance and your quiet insistence that I keep going.

To my children, Prathee and Shavi, my teachers in ways they will only understand when they are much older. You remind me that tenderness can be radical, that accountability makes love sharper, and that the world must be shaped, not simply inherited. Your presence chiselled me into someone capable of writing these poems, even when the writing demanded that I confront old wounds. Thank you for expanding my heart's vocabulary.

Deepest gratitude to my friends, who stayed through the unravelling, listened without asking me to soften, and held me steady in the moments these poems were still finding their breath.

This book is dedicated to women everywhere who walk through conflict, displacement, and violence, not as footnotes to war but as the ones who carry families, communities, and memories on their backs. To the women who have endured the weight of systems built to erase them, who have buried children, crossed borders, or rebuilt their lives from the ashes of decisions made by men holding guns or power. To the women who resist in ways the world rarely recognises—through survival, through stubborn love, or through the simple act of continuing to breathe.

To the women whose bodies became battlegrounds, whose stories were swallowed by shame not of their making. To the women who fled home with nothing but their name and their rage. To the women who stitched their dignity back together, thread by trembling thread. To the women who lost faith and found it again in themselves. To the women who prayed to goddesses, or to no one at all, but still rose.

These poems draw on Kali not as a deity but as a metaphor for refusal, for rebirth, for the audacity to live after devastation. They are written for every woman who has ever held both fury and gentleness in the same breath, who has learned to destroy what diminishes her and nurture what sets her free.

This book is for you. May you find your own fire in these pages, and may it remind you that even in the darkest nights, there is a pulse inside you that refuses to surrender.

I.
THE FIRST VISITATION

(Childhood dream memories,
the first trembling awareness of the Goddess)

Encounter with Kali I: The Child Who Saw Her

He runs wild through my parents' home,
barefoot, electric, alive,
a comet made of giggles and mischief,
a chubby bundle of joy.
His laughter bounces off the walls,
and we, tired gods in mortal bodies,
chase behind him with warnings,
like prayers falling from faithless lips.

'Stop!'
'You'll fall!'
'Careful!'

But he keeps running.
He doesn't know danger;
he only hears joy.

Then
he veers left
into the altar room—
that quiet square of incense and stillness,
a space that smells of sandalwood and surrender.

We follow,
and then—
the scream.

Not of pain,
not quite fear,
but something else sharp—
something I still can't name.

He's standing in front of the altar,
his little chest rising like storm waves,
his finger pressed to his mouth.

'Ssshhhh,' he says,
his voice a whisper wrapped in soft awe.

'What is it, baby?' we ask,
half-smiling, half-alarmed.

He points to her and says:
'She was here. Full of gold.
She looked at me and said "ssshhhh".'

Again, he presses his tiny finger over his lips,
as if relaying instructions
from a realm we have forgotten how to visit.

We look at the altar—
Kali, calm and black,
eyes like eclipses,
a playful smile,
riding a lion.
No wrath, no fury,
but something in the room shifts.

Like breath being held,
like memory re-entering the body,
like time rewinding.

We say nothing.
My son goes back to running,
the moment already dissolving behind him
like sugar in warm milk.

But I know what I saw—
not with my eyes,
but with something older.

She was there.
She is here.
And she spoke to my child first.

Encounter with Kali II: The Dream at Kanthan

It happened many years after I left *Kanthan,*
after the *darshan* that left my body buzzing for days,
after I touched the stone threshold of her temple
and left feeling watched.

She came to me in a dream,
not with thunder
but in silence as thick as honey.
Her face was shadowed at first,
as if the world wasn't ready yet.
Then slowly, deliberately,
she lifted her head.

Kali.

No skulls. No tongue. No terror.
Just gold. Endless, glistening gold—
anklets, bangles, collarbones dipped in it.
Her eyes, blacker than river mud,
met mine without flinching.

She was so beautiful
I forgot where I was.
Her body was strong, heavy, wild—
not flawless
but formed of everything I was told not to become.

And before I could stop myself,
before shame could catch up with desire,

I whispered,
'I want to touch you.'
Not with hands
but with everything I never dared to name.

She didn't speak.
She stepped closer.
The ground did not shake;
my chest did.

I didn't know whether I wanted to fall to my knees,
press my forehead to hers,
or crawl inside her skin and disappear.

'Is this wrong?' I asked.

She touched my face,
her fingers cool and firm.
'No. This is remembering,'
she said.

And I did—
in a rush,
a thousand lives of searching, of fighting her, of being her.

I thought: Maybe we were lovers once,
maybe I was her priestess,
or the enemy she spared,
or her child,
or her mother—
or all of them at once.

We sat together on the floor of the dream,
no temple, no body, no rules,
just the two of us
and the weight of everything unsaid.

We didn't speak of grief,
but I could feel her hand on the part of me
that still carried my mother's death like a stone.

We didn't speak of desire,
but I could feel her breath where my hunger lived.
We didn't speak of guilt,
but she looked at me as if she knew every time I'd called
myself too much.

'I am you,' she said,
'on the days you burn,
on the nights you feel everything too deeply,
when you snap, when you cry in the shower,
when you hold your lover too hard,
when you walk away without explaining.'

I wanted to ask how to hold it all.
She placed a hand over my chest.
'You already are,' she said.

When I woke up,
my body was still trembling,
not in fear
but in recognition.

Encounter with Kali III: The Unlearning

She laughs.
'Hello,' she says, dragging the word like silk between teeth.
'Is that how you like to be greeted?'
Her joy is dangerous. Full-bodied. Hilarious. Divine.
And her breasts,
I try not to stare,
but they fill the room like answers I don't yet deserve.

She says my name like we've fucked before,
like we were lovers in some dusky, moonlit *yuga,*
talking about revolution between gulps of mango juice
and smearing sandalwood on each other's throats.
I don't ask.
I just wonder:
Did we love like that?
Did I trace the curve of her breast with a prayer once?

'I'm flustered,' I say. 'There's too much on my plate.'
I talk like a woman unravelling.
I want clarity. I want sleep. I want to fight.
I want her to tell me I'm important,
that this burn in my chest is purpose, not panic.

She tilts her head. 'Why do you do so much?'
I tell her about the artists,
the project,
the belief in young minds,
the fear of being left behind,
the ego, the performance, the fear of aging out of relevance.

She listens like she already knows.
She does.

'Pause,' she says.
I do.
'Are you reflecting?'
I nod.
I tell her about the letter to Bahma, whose mother is slipping away.
It sounded too philosophical,
too composed.
'I feel like a fuckwit,' I say.

She doesn't flinch.
'You didn't write that. Something else did. It came through you.'

She always says so,
that I'm a channel,
that every word I spit out,
every breakdown, every swell of insight
is just energy taking form.

I roll my eyes.
She grins.
I curse.
She laughs like thunder wrapped in honey.

I want to fight her.
I want her arms around me.
I want to sob into her breastbone until time ends.

She calls me 'baby'.
And suddenly, I am eight
and fifty
and ageless.

'There is no good or bad,' she says.
'Only experiences.'
'Like death?'
'Like death.'

'Like burnout?'

'Like choosing the same fire over and over
until your skin remembers how to heal.'

I cry.
She watches,
not cruelly,
just with the full weight of a woman who has witnessed
centuries of grief turned to bone.

She tells me everything passes.
She tells me love and sadness are the same creature,
that the ache of losing someone
is the echo of loving them well.

'You're thinking of him,' she says.
I nod.
She doesn't need to ask.
She sees it all—
the joy in his breath, the ache in his absence,
how my bipolar sharpens around him like glass around light.

'If I may suggest…' she begins.
I cut her off.
'Since when have you become so polite?'

She smirks.
'If I may suggest, you stay still,
breathe,
be the eye of the storm.'

I whisper, 'Kali.'

She replies,
'Nothing happens *to* you, baby.
Everything happens *for* you.'

She tells me I am rewriting my life each time I notice,
each time I stay instead of escape,
each time I burn but choose not to ash.

She tells me she loves me.
She doesn't need to,
but she does.

I don't ask if she's real.
I ask if I ever was
before her.

Encounter with Kali IV: The Return

She came again,
not in a dream this time,
not naked, golden, thunderous.
No altar,
no fire,
just the edge of my kitchen sink.

I was peeling ginger,
half-listening to the news,
half-scrolling through grief—
a picture of a woman raped in war,
a boy amid rubble,
a UN report no one would read.

And then,
the air thickened.
The ginger slipped from my hand.
I looked up
and there she was,
leaning against the fridge,
arms crossed,
in a sari that looked like ash.

'You burn yourself too clean,' she said.

I didn't reply.
I was too tired to talk back to divinity,
too raw to explain my exhaustion.
She already knew.

‘Still trying to save the world?’
she asked,
arching one perfect brow.

‘I’m trying to stay upright,’ I said.

She walked over slowly,
barefoot on tile,
the sound of anklets like breath against bone.
‘You’re grieving,’ she said.
‘For the world. For yourself.’
I nodded.
‘It feels endless.’

She sat beside me on the floor,
folded her legs,
and rested her chin on her hand.
‘You think I don’t grieve?’
she asked, eyes locked on mine.
‘I carry oceans in this body.
I’ve watched mothers bury children
with no time to name them.
I’ve watched forests scream.
I’ve drowned in blood.
And I’ve danced anyway.’

I closed my eyes.
I didn’t want answers.
I wanted permission
to be broken
and still beautiful.

She reached for my hand,
held it.

'Take a breath,' she said.
So I did.
And with it came the smallest flicker—
not peace
but possibility.

'You don't have to fix it all,' she said.
'You just have to be here
to behold the unbearable without shutting your eyes,
to keep your heart soft
even when it hurts,
to live fully,
and rest,
and eat fruit in the sun,
and come,
and cry,
and scream, if you must.'

I leaned into her shoulder,
let my head rest against the goddess.

'Even if I do nothing?' I asked.
'Even if I collapse?'
'Especially then,' she whispered.
'You're not here to be useful.
You're here to be alive.'

Encounter with Kali V: Letter to the Dark Mother

Ma,

I write this from the floor,
not because I've collapsed
but because it feels right to meet you here,
ground to ground,
body to Earth.
You taught me this.

I am not broken, not exactly.
Just between things,
A breath before the next version of myself.
You know how that goes.

You've watched me unravel,
stretch, flinch, resist, return.
You've moved through every version of me—
the girl screaming 'Czechoslovakia' like a spell
to feel history in her throat,
to remember where her soul had burned before,
the child who somehow knew
she'd died in a Polish camp,
that the smell of smoke meant more than fear.

You've danced in my blood
when I was a barefoot gypsy in another life,
brown-skinned, defiant,
laughing through ash,
with bells on my ankles

and secrets behind my eyes.
I think you were in me then too,
in the boldness,
in the wild joy I carried like a blade.

You're in me now, too.
Even when my bank account sighs,
even when I pace the kitchen, whispering prayers
into the steam of tea,
even when I cry over spreadsheets, sagging ceilings,
and the wild, irrational love I feel for a world that breaks
itself daily.

I've become a lightworker, Ma,
the kind that isn't performative
the kind that sees into shadows
and doesn't flinch.
I understand now:
Unconditional love is not softness.
It is fierce.
It is boundary-less.
It roars.

I've stopped shrinking.
I say no now, more often than before.
I look men in the eye
and do not flinch when they blink first.
I honour my hunger
for solitude, for connection, for clarity.
I no longer feel guilty
for wanting things
that are mine to want.

You've made me wise,
not in the way people celebrate
but in the way women survive,
with cracked hands,
with humour sharp as glass,
with altars built in cluttered kitchens
and poems written at 3am
when the spirit won't sleep.

I still struggle,
but I am no longer lost.

I am rooted.
I am guided.
And in my worst moments,
I can still feel you,
in the ache between my shoulder blades,
in the heat behind my eyes,
in the unshakeable knowing that
this pain, too, is part of the dance.

One day, I will go to Mexico
and find the witches who hum to the moon,
the ones who know stories I've forgotten,
the ones who call the winds by name.

And they will recognise me,
not because I'll tell them who I am
but because they'll feel you in me,
just like I do.

Thank you for not being gentle with me.
Thank you for staying, even when I raged.
Thank you for loving me in the language of fire
and for showing me that destruction
can also be sacred.

I'll keep walking.
I'll keep listening.
And when I forget who I am,
I know you'll send a crow, a scent, or a sentence
to bring me back.

In devotion, in defiance, in love,
always yours,
M

II.
WOMEN WHO BURN AND RISE

(Survival, girlhood, patriarchy, violence, and the fight to reclaim self).

Kali's Daughters

The scent of crushed neem leaves and gunpowder hangs thick as grandmothers kneel in the dirt, grinding rebellion into paste. Their mortar and pestle, once tools for preparing medicine, now pound bullet casings into talismans. The oldest ones remember that before temples confined her, Kali ran wild through these villages, her necklace of skulls clattering like monsoon rain on tin roofs.

In the city, a banker's silk blouse sticks to her back as she burns ledgers in the parking garage. The flames turn years of 'adjusted' salaries to black snow. The revolution smells like the acrid sting of *sindoor* burning in corporate boardrooms, where women now stand with bare feet on polished tables, their toe rings leaving crescent-shaped dents in imported mahogany. It sounds like grandmothers snapping their glass bangles deliberately, not in mourning but to use the shards to carve new runes into the walls of Parliament.

Midwives deliver babies with one hand and pamphlets with the other. The birth cord isn't cut; it's braided into rope. Girls smear red vermillion powder, not in hair partings but across cheekbones like war paint.

The dead walk with us. You can see them in the flicker of streetlights during blackouts—great-great-grandmothers, who drowned with stones tied to their feet, now hovering behind their descendants, whispering which trail of corrupt money to follow, the taste of their vengeance, bitter gourd and tamarind.

At midnight kitchens, women bake *rotis* laced with the ashes of burned dowry agreements. The first bite makes your gums bleed truth: We remember every daughter burnt alive, every womb carved open for being 'too slow' to bear sons, every 'suicide' note written in a man's handwriting. The revolution will be served hot, with sides of justice and extra spite.

She appears where they least expect—in the static of hijacked broadcasts, Kali's image pixelating across screens, and in the warped reflection of a bureaucrat's polished shoes as a sweeper 'accidentally' spills menstrual blood on them.

We tried petitions. You called it nagging.

We tried protests. You called it PMS.

And so now, the goddess wears many faces—the bar girl who spikes drinks with truth serum; the *Dalit* grandmother who breaks entire caste systems by twiddling her thumbs; a student whose backpack is full of 'theory' that's really a manifesto.

We are Kali's daughters…..We are the daughters of the fire you tried to drown in holy water.

Our rebellion is the knife in the *mithai* box, the curse in the blessing, the widow's white *sari* dyed red in your halls of power.

You gave us chains, we made them into a bridge. Now, watch us cross.

The War Kite

It's 6.34 pm on a Tuesday. She is at the kitchen sink, wrist-deep in cold water, washing carrots. And then, without warning, she crashes—not slips but falls, as if yanked by something older than gravity. Her knees slam down, the linoleum moans, a tremor ripples through the tile, and her breath stops mid-inhale. When she comes to, pain slices through her side each time the little boy tugs, wild and relentless.

The boy holds the string of what *Kuala Emas* calls the smartest kite in the sky. His hands are quick, almost divine. His fingers summon shapes and myth from the air, painting kites with a kind of madness only born, never taught. They sell for hundreds, but none are like this one.

This kite is laced in gold, silver, and black and etched with faces and stories from twelve years of the boy's memory or maybe from lifetimes before that. He calls it Sayang, a pet name, a cradle word. But this kite is not Sayang.

It is fury wrapped in cloth. It is wind-lashed bone and bitten tongue. It is tired of dancing prettily in the air for a child who does not see its rage, of the forced pirouettes, of being made to compete for beauty when it was born for battle. It is Kali's tongue, long, blood-soaked, defiant, flapping in the monsoon sky.

The kite hates the shimmer of gold on its skin, the femininity forced upon it. It dreams of the colour of ash, of night, of a tooth broken in revolt. It snarls at the name 'Sayang'. It prefers Hang Jebat, the traitor, warrior, godless loyalist. It does not float; it fights, against the wind, against the name, against the boy.

But how does one declare war when one's mouth is stitched with string? Or when one has no words in the boy's language to say: 'I am not what you think I am. I am not your pretty plaything. I am Kali's child. I am holy rage in silk.'

At night, the kite dreams of severing its string, of unspooling into the jungle, of wrapping itself around the moon and howling through the treetops, of war drums, of goddesses with necklaces made of heads and swords still wet from judgement. It dreams of a sky not bound by boyhood fantasies but of storm-light and scream.

It remembers, perhaps, being something else before this life—a sword, a banner, a curse whispered by women who had lost everything but their sanity. Maybe once it was Kali's garment, flung from the battlefield, still warm with divine rage. And now, it's here, mistaken for a child's companion, a painted toy.

It rages not because it hates the boy but because it remembers the old blood. It remembers what it was to be feared, to be worshipped, to be something a man would bow before and beg not to be devoured. Now, it is reduced to second-place trophies and sulking silences. This is not living; this is desecration.

Sometimes the wind is so strong that it feels almost free. Those are the moments it screams its name into the sky, hoping someone will hear it. Not Sayang, not darling, not girl but the real name, the one that tears open sky- veins and drowns entire empires in fire. But the boy only laughs when it jerks too hard and calls it 'naughty'.

The kite weeps when it must return. It collapses into itself like a warrior made to wear perfume. The boy, unaware, coils the string lovingly, thinking he understands love. But love is not ownership.

Beneath the cloud line of the state, behind the places of worship and market stalls, are stories that never fly—girls married off before their breasts have bloomed, some traded for dowries, others given away because feeding them meant less rice for the rest. The kite has heard whispers from rooftops and mangroves: an eleven-year-old with a man thrice her age, a child forced to call her rapist 'husband', a silence sanctified in the name of faith.

It is no accident that the kite carries fury in its ribs. It has been sewn from scraps of those same wedding garments, their lace now stiff with memory. It was lifted by hands belonging to a boy who doesn't yet know what's been buried in the soil he walks on. His village is not poor in prayer but in justice, in safety, in voices that say no and mean it. Some wounds do not bleed but fester into myth.

And so, the kite flies not for sport but for vengeance. It spirals through the sky like a black omen, watching over homes where shame sleeps between father and daughter, where hunger dresses itself as discipline, where the holy tongue has been trained to call obedience a virtue. But Kali remembers. And through the kite, she returns.

Kali, Not Your Godmen

Hare Rama, Hare Krishna!
Hail Rama, hail Krishna!
These chants choke me.
They taste like sanctified ash in my mouth,
sweet only to those who've never had their bodies
sliced by scriptures.

Lord Rama: blue-skinned, obedient, and beautiful.
Surpanaka dares to want him.
She is punished not for the lust, but for her ugliness.
His brother hacks off her nose,
and people call it divine justice.
Sita crosses a line—Rama's line—
and is blamed for everything that follows.
Why do even gods write the rules in a man's hand?

Lord Krishna: trickster, thief of hearts and clothes.
He watches women bathe, laughs from the trees,
steals their saris like it's foreplay.
Would you call that man your ideal son-in-law?
A voyeur- turned- deity,
and still, his perversion is made poetic
because he 'loves' Radha,
a married woman.
But wait…they say Ayan, her husband, is just Krishna in costume
and not just for Halloween.
But when did I become a whore?

Rama forces Sita to walk through fire
not for him
but for the crowd.
'I believe you,' he says.
'But they need proof.'
Would you trust a man who makes you burn
just to calm the gossip?
And still, they chant his name.

All these men with halos,
cowards hiding behind epics.

But Kali…
She doesn't beg for belief.
She doesn't seduce.
She storms.
She halts Shiva's destruction with a single footfall.
She makes no apologies.
No chastity tests.
No passive smiles.
And still, no one calls her a slut.
They wouldn't dare.
Shiva isn't even her husband in most re-telling;
he's just the man beneath her foot.

Isn't it time to change these other stories?
We've swallowed too many of them whole,
tales twisted to glorify obedience,
myths soaked in patriarchy and passed off as moral truth.
These aren't epics; they're instruction manuals
on how to tame women.
We owe it to ourselves

to rip the sacred from the sexist,
to write new legends that don't reek of control.
Because what's divine about making women bleed
just to prove they're pure?

This is my worship:
A red sari at midnight,
gold-bordered *zari* like flames,
kohl like war paint,
a *bindi* like a third eye, unblinking.
I become Kali.

I met her twice before
while giving birth,
my body twisting, unrecognisable,
screaming, swearing, soaked in blood and power.
In the eye of that storm,
there was a silence more sacred
than any hymn
for my unborn child.

Kali is not noise.
She is stillness in movement.

Can all women wake her?
Can we start roaring,
own the space we were told to shrink in,
write with ink and fury,
dance like no one's watching?
Can we wear the wind
like a crown?

Blood Money

Tuesday, 6:43pm.
Trilokha is in a makeshift tent stitched together with scraps—
gunny sack corners, faded plastic, the last shreds of modesty.
Summer in Bhopal is a beast with no skin.
The air stinks of heat and men.
Her father is missing again.
'Probably face down in a drain, drunk off his worthless ass,'
she spits.

She's angry, yes. But fear lingers too.
What if he's dead?
What if she's alone in this godforsaken circus—
hair still wet, skin sticky, wrapped in her father's *dhoti,*
no towel, no privacy, no time?
Luxury is for gods,
for people who don't hang from ropes
and eat hope for breakfast.

They call her 'Mahalakshmi'
because of her smouldering eyes, her chocolate skin.
Irony is a cruel thing.
The goddess of wealth has never once glanced in their
direction.
Trilokha flies through air, walks on wires, flips over death.
Her father juggles flaming knives and pretends to tame lions.
Still, they can barely eat.
The circus owner—fat, rotting, always sweating—
owns their lives like he owns their debts.

If she lets him touch her,
her father's loans would vanish.
They might even have enough to leave.
But Trilokha would rather burn.

The bell rings.
She scrambles into her costume—
obscene yellow sequins, pants stitched too tight,
red lipstick like blood across her mouth,
a smile trained into place.
Kumar, the boy who kisses her like she's salvation,
would say her lips taste like fire.
He trains monkeys to dance.
He doesn't know how to read, but he knows how to need.
Their future is a fog of debt and desperation.

The second bell screams.
She bolts down the corridor.
Her stomach snarls at the thought of watery *dhal*
and translucent *chappati.*
She turns a corner.
A hand grabs her,
a slap cracks across her face.
Her breath catches.
The smell hits first.
She knows that breath,
that filth, that hunger.

He rips. She fights. He tears. She screams.
But the corridor is black,
and the world outside is even darker.

Elsewhere,
her father laughs with other cowards,
his pockets heavy with rupees that stink of her blood.
Does he know what she paid?
Would he care if he did?

But there's someone else watching,
someone older than gods, wilder than men.
Her name is Kali.
She hears the breathlessness in Trilokha's throat,
the prayer that never makes it past her tongue.
She does not ask for permission to enter.
She does not wait to be worshipped.

Kali comes with her tongue out,
dripping red.
She wears her rage like jewellery.
And when she sees Trilokha's torn clothes,
when she sees her still fighting,
she doesn't weep.
She laughs,
not in mockery
but in redemption

Kali, dark as the moonless night,
does not come to save.
She comes to ignite.
And in that moment,
as the man claws at Trilokh,
as his sweat drips onto her cheek,
something shifts.

Trilokha bites…hard.
His scream pierces the air.

The man staggers back, bleeding.
And Trilokha, bleeding too, stands.
Not untouched. Not unharmed.
But unbroken.
Kali stands beside her, unseen by others,
A silent twin,
a black flame in a yellow sequinned costume.

Trilokha walks to the ring.
She mounts the rope.
And flies.

My Vagina is Dry as a Desert

My vagina is dry as a desert, not from lack of desire but from drought, a season-less silence, the kind that follows fire, exile, and a thousand betrayals, the kind of aridity not even gods can name, unless they have known war.

I no longer bleed, not because I've aged but because I have unlearned softness. I have armoured my thighs with salt and bone. This is a stillness that came after the rage, after the invasions, after the hands that took without asking and the tongues that lied. It is not shame that dried me; it is history.

I used to be a river. I remember her well. She moved through me, wild, uncontained, whispering secrets to the moon. But they mutilated me with terror, severing the flow violently, ritualistically, until I learned to fear my own wetness.

But Kali walks in, smelling of ash and jasmine, always barefoot, always ferocious, always raw. She doesn't knock. She doesn't ask for permission. She does not bring rain but rupture. She does not ask if I am ready. She reopens my lesions so they can finally breathe. She reminds me I am real. She sits between my legs and hums until she hears my ancestors, buried alive.

'You are not broken,' she says. 'You are resting. You are remembering.'

Kali touches the scorched folds of me, not as a healer but as a witness. She names every scar, every silence, every ending as a sacred ritual. She reminds me that even the absence of sound can be a spell, that withdrawal can be resistance, that not all softness must survive to be sacred. Her presence peels back shame like dead bark. My body, long silenced, begins to murmur again, low, volcanic, dangerous, a sound older than language.

This desert holds secrets—bones of grandmothers, burnt hymns, aborted dreams of girls who never got to name themselves. But slowly, I begin to hear the voices in the dust. Sisters. Warriors. Ghosts. The ones who bled out under boots. The ones who screamed into pillows. The ones who stitched their dignity back together, one defiant breath at a time. They speak through me now. I carry them all, not as burden but as blood.

Kali does not promise healing; she promises fire. And sometimes, fire is the only way the rain remembers how to fall.

The first tear is not moisture; it is memory. The second is anger. By the third, something in me shifts, a reminder that I am not only what was done to me but also what rose in the aftermath. I am the echo and the curse. I am the seed in cracked clay, waiting for the storm of my own making. And when it comes, I will bloom in the ruins.

This world does not know how to hold women who do not apologise, who do not hide their rage in perfume, who bleed without permission. But I have learned to carry my fury like a torch not a wound.

There are temples within me they tried to desecrate, but my bones remember the architecture. My breath rebuilds altars from the debris. Every moan, every scream, every unspoken prayer is holy. Every time I survive, I become less afraid of the power I carry.

And so, Kali does not walk alone anymore. I walk with her. We wear our wrath like silk, our scars like scripture. We are not here to be healed. We are here to be heard. And we are not waiting for permission.

III.
THE MOMO SCRIPTURES

(A philosophical, playful, cutting interrogation of purity, belief, and truth)

AumMomoNamah: The Sermon of the Soft-Bellied Sage

(*Delivered from the Steps of the Mango Tree)*

O devotees, O disciples, O dazed daughters of *dharma*!
Listen not with your ears but with your loins.
No! No! With your hearts!
(That slipped out like *ghee* in summer.)

I, Pundit Momo, round as a blessing, soft as a chewed *paan,*
walk not lightly upon this earth.
I thud with purpose.
I wobble with wisdom.
I jiggle with joy, for I am full,
full of divine carbs and confusing urges.

They call me Motu, in that sweet Hindustani way.
Chubby, yes. But was not Ganesha blessed with a belly?
Was not the Buddha fat with enlightenment?

Then why, O why, do women follow me like ants to *gulab jamun*?
I did not ask for this.
I chant. I fast. I even 'gym-ed' once.
Still, their eyes undress my soul.

Their *saris* whisper my name: 'Momo… Momo…'
Even the married ones,
especially the married ones.
What is this curse of charisma, what cruel prank of the cosmos?

But there is one…
One whose shadow passed like a monsoon breeze.
Not flesh but fire,
not smile but spell.

Kali, short for Kaliammah.

Wife of Shiva, keeper of flames,
burner of bodies, eater of legends.
Why is beauty wrapped in ashes?
Why does the scent of sandalwood remind me of her?

Today, I go,
not as learned,
not as a *pundit,*
but as a man.
May the gods forgive me.
May my wife not stay up.
May my desire be temporary.

The House of Ash and Honey

(From the Secret Scrolls of the Soft-Bellied Sage)

O disciples!
There are moments when the soul trembles,
not from fear
but from recognition,
from the memory of a body you've never touched,
a voice you've never heard
but which cracks open the clay of lifetimes.

She opened the door
before I knocked.
Did she know I'd come
or had she summoned me in silence,
chanting my name into the smoke of the cremation fires?

Kaliammah.

Her name tastes like burnt cloves and nectar.
Her breasts spoke first,
then her eyes,
then the roughness of her voice,
as if the forest itself had spoken through a woman's throat.
'I have waited for you through different lifetimes. And here you are, finally.'

O disciples!
What does a *pundit* do
when a goddess says she's waited for him?

I, who dodged lovers like monkeys dodge coconuts,
I, who meditated in mango groves to escape lust,
I, who wore loose robes to hide my rising afflictions,
stood there, hard with confusion.

'Waited for me?' I asked,
like a goat questioning thunder.

She touched my wrist.
The air around us flickered.
Her house smelled of *ghee*, incense, and something older—
ash and honey,
death and smoke.

I remembered not my mantras,
not my sacred verses,
only the shape of her mouth
as she spoke no words
and still told me everything.

O devotees, O damp-eyed truth-seekers!
Beware of the woman who waits at the window!
She may not want your love;
she may want your undoing.
And yet, I went in.
I chose to go in.
And as the door closed behind me,
I did not hear the latch
but the slow crack of an old vow breaking.

Forgive me, Apsara, my other half!
Forgive me, gods of garlic and restraint!

For tonight, I am not Momo, the Pundit.
I am just Momo,
a man meeting his fire.

The Mirror of the Flame

(The Final Realisation of the Soft-Bellied Sage)

O listeners!
Let me now speak,
not as a man of flesh but of fire,
Not as husband, nor lover,
but as one who stood at the door of illusion
and walked through.

The room was dim,
the bedsheets untouched.
The incense curled like question marks in the air.
Kaliammah touched my chest
not with lust but with knowing.

She did not undress me.
She undressed my hunger,
held it in her palm like a ripe fruit and said,
'Bite not into me, Momo.
Bite into your longing.
I am not your lover. I am your flame.'

And then, like smoke after a pyre,
she vanished.

O disciples! She was never there!
Not truly.
Not in skin,
not in breath.

She was *Maya,*
the divine illusion who dresses herself in longing
so we may find the fire inside the cave.

And I wept.

I wept not because I lost her
but because I had found myself,
the part of me I buried beneath sermons, sweets, and
celibacy.

The internal Kali,
the wild, untamed, dark goddess
who dances behind my ribs
and eats my falsehoods raw.

She was the one who waited.
She was the one who pulled me in.
She was the mirror,
and I was the moth.

O seekers of truth!
Desire is not sin;
desire is a compass.
It points not to the body of another
but to the unloved corners of yourself.

I return now to Apsara,
not a liar,
not a lecher,
but a man who has met his shadow and bowed.

From this day on,
I will not preach escape;
I will preach encounter.
Meet your hunger.
Meet your fear.
Meet your Kali.

And when you do,
laugh like Ganesha,
dance like Shiva,
and if you must,
wobble like me.

IV.
GHOSTS, GIRLS, AND LINEAGE

(Family, heritage, and inherited grief,
the lines between mothers and daughters)

The Price of a Girl

It is a narrow street, with litter scattered like dead prayers. The incense is cheap, failing to cover the sweat, the cigarette breath, and the stench of men. Zari, all bones and hunger, leans against a cracked wall, her spine a question no one wants to answer.

'*Arre, chalo yaar*, come with me. I'll take care of you,' says Didi in a gravelly voice, her neck like tree bark, smile like a bruise.

That was two weeks ago. Zari remembers the banana peel and temple gate, her mouth too dry to cry. Her mother died birthing her. Her father called her the final curse. He sold her like she was an unbearable burden for three thousand rupees and a bottle of country liquor. The truck driver said nothing. He played a Bhojpuri song on repeat as if it were a survival mantra, chain-smoked, and spat red out the window. She never saw her village again.

Now, she can hear Didi, sugar-laced venom one moment, thunderclap the next, her footsteps like warning shots. Today, all storm.

'Get Zari ready for tonight,' she snaps. Hands strip her dress like it has never belonged to her. She stands: eight years old, ribs sharp as prayer flags. 'You are our Mahalakshmi,' Didi says, voice low, almost reverent. A goddess, they say, to be worshipped by men with rotting mouths, to bring money. That's what makes her divine.

The bathroom tiles sting her soles. The water is like ice. She doesn't flinch. Silence is safer than sound. The women scrub her like a dirty dish.

A green sari is pulled from a plastic bag, soft as deception. 'Nice, *na*?' someone says.

They wrap her like a gift meant to be unwrapped—black *kohl,* red *bindi*, her lips painted in someone else's story.

Bangles jingle. The candle flickers. The rustle of silk is too loud. They push her into a dim room, the air thick with incense. She gags on memory: urine-soaked alleyways, torn slippers, the stomach's lonely growl.

Her eyes find the sweets—*laddoos, jalebi, halwa* on a silver tray. 'You can eat later,' one woman says. That word *later* tastes like a lie.

She waits. Time curls and unravels. Then comes the knock. Didi enters, the shadow of a man behind her. 'You'll do what he says,' Didi says, not cruel, not kind, just done.

He steps forward, big, belly over belt, mouth red from chewing *paan*. He smells like every man who's ever taken too much. Zari looks down. Faint, fleeting memory clouds her eyes.

And then, he lunges. The sari tears at her waist. A hand crushes her chest, pain blooming like poison. She runs. '*Darwaza kholo*!' Her fists pound wood. There's no one to open the door. A hand pulls her hair, followed by a slap, sharp, blinding. Then another. Her body caves. He lifts her like a rag and tosses her on to the bed.

She's half-conscious, half-alive. She screams once more, as something ancient splits inside her, not just skin but the last corner of childhood.

What He Doesn't Know (From Zari)

He didn't know I remembered
the way his fingers gripped my ankle when
I was small and crying,
the way he once called me a curse in a cracked whisper,
blaming me for her death before I'd even learned to speak.

He didn't know it was me,
green sari, red lips.
The child he tossed like a coin
now returned to him as currency.

He didn't know what it means to carry
a scream inside your ribs
for eight years,
to learn silence not as peace
but as survival.

He didn't know that I wasn't just bleeding;
I was becoming.

Because on the night he pressed his weight against me,
the same weight that once lifted me as a baby,
the same stench I once called father,
I felt something else enter the room.

Not fear,
not death.
Kali.

She arrived without footsteps,
black-skinned and brilliant.
Her tongue tasted of iron and rage,
her eyes two full moons of judgement.

She didn't comfort me,
she didn't cradle me.
She watched.

And when I screamed,
she screamed too,
a sound that cracked the ceiling.
The candle blew out.

I lay still. Not limp. Not defeated.
Still, like the sea before a storm.
She bent down, kissed my forehead,
and whispered, 'This is not how your story ends.'

He walked out that night,
buttoning up shame without knowing its name.
I stayed behind,
with a body torn
but a spirit stitched with fire.

I wait now,
not for rescue,
not for love,

but for the next breath of power
I will call my own.

He doesn't know
that his daughter is gone,
and in her place,
a goddess is learning
how to rise
and how to strike.

Blue

Once, in the dense mist of the forgotten edge of maps, where incense meets gunpowder and jasmine weeps into stone, a high-caste Indian tree took root in the middle of a Chinese graveyard.

No one knows how her seed landed there. It was carried, perhaps, by a reckless monsoon wind or dropped by a bird exiled from two worlds. She grew straight and tall, proud of her lineage: daughter of Brahmins, granddaughter of banyans that once shaded the feet of saints. Her skin bore the markings of old Sanskrit verses, and her sap bled turmeric and sandalwood.

The Chinese dead welcomed her quietly. Their bones did not mind her arrogance. Their gravestones hummed lullabies in Mandarin when the wind passed through her branches. Over time, the tree stopped chanting her mantras so loudly. She listened. She observed.

One dusk, she fell in love, not with another majestic tree but with a wandering, wild, weird-looking hunk from the riverbank. He was lower-born, uncultivated. His roots tangled with weeds. But his shadow danced, and he whispered stories of rebellion. She bent slightly towards him. The graveyard sighed. The couple entwined.

Her ancestors watched from the heavens, horrified. A daughter of their lineage marrying beneath her caste, in the land of ghosts? They cursed her, with the slow cruelty of those who believe in purity above all. 'You will break,' they whispered. 'In love. In labour.'

And she did.

During the longest lunar eclipse, under a sky drained of all colour, she split open with pain. Her fruit dropped too early. Her limbs withered in agony. She died giving birth to a sapling unlike any ever seen.

The child had wild, coiled leaves that refused to grow straight, a trunk with unapologetic curves, and bark the hue of indigo smoke. The graveyard stirred, and the Chinese spirits wept, not in mourning but awe. Her mother, with her final breath, named her Blue.

Blue grew like no tree before her. She cracked stone with her roots. She laughed when lightning struck. She bore fruit that made women dream in shades their grandmothers were not allowed to name. Some called her a witch, others, divine.

In her limbs lived the spirit of Kali: the dark mother, the devourer of illusion, the goddess of teeth and time, not the soft god of comfort but the fierce one who dances on corpses and wears a necklace of severed lies. Blue, like Kali, did not ask permission to exist.

She carried rage without apology and love without condition. She did not bloom in spring like other trees but in aftermaths. Her flowers opened in warzones and funerals. She fed the forgotten and swallowed the shame of women who had no names left. In every storm, her leaves sang: *I am not your ruin; I am your reckoning.*

Blue became a pilgrimage site, not for the devout but for the disobedient. Women who had once buried their tongues came barefoot, smearing their foreheads with her husk. Widows whispered secrets to her bark. Daughters, too wild for dowries, braided her fallen leaves into their hair. Even monks came—those who had renounced the world but never its injustices—and sat beneath her, wordless, watching her shadow stretch beyond the laws of men.

One spring, when the river swallowed half the borderland,

Blue stood firm and nourished refugees with sour fruit and strange hope.

She ensured no child who slept beneath her boughs ever had the same nightmare twice. She rewrote dreams, leaf by leaf, into stories of resistance, where girls never married their rapists and boys wept freely under the stars.

But Blue was not without enemies. Officials came with chainsaws and bulldozers, declaring her invasive, illegal, and unregistered. They called her a threat to national identity. But when they tried to cut her down, her roots bled ink that stained their boots and wrote poems across the earth. Every time a blade touched her trunk, someone far away told the truth.

Blue doesn't appear on maps, though her name is sung at borders and in the belly of prisons, a tree with no country but a thousand stories. Some say she grows taller each time a girl says no, when a caste is broken, or a god is questioned. She is not holy because she is worshipped; she is sacred because she survived.

And so, she stands, somewhere between memory and myth, a tree born of scandal and miracle, a tree that dared to grow in a graveyard and name herself, a tree that reminds the world that from death, from disgrace, from curses can come the divine.

To the Woman Told to Stay Silent

They taught you to keep your head down,
to serve tea with a smile,
to swallow your anger like bitter medicine.

They said a 'good woman' endures…
Endures a man who yells, who drinks, who hits,
endures a family that tells her, 'Be patient, that's just how men are,'
endures a life of doing, giving, and being forgotten.

But listen to me, sister!
There is a fire inside you.
It is older than all their rules.
It is older than their temples, their laws, their villages.

That fire has a name.
Some call her Kali, the wild mother who dances on the ruins of lies.
Some call her freedom.
Some call her justice.
But really, she is just you,
the real you, before they broke your back with shame and fear.

You don't need to read big books to know this.
You already feel it in your bones every time you ask,
'Is this all my life will be?'
You already know it every time you stay awake at night, thinking,

'I was meant for more.'
Kali doesn't sit in the sky waiting for prayers.
She lives in the woman who says no.
She lives in the woman who says, I deserve better.
She lives in the woman who leaves a bad marriage, even when everyone tells her not to.
She lives in the woman who feeds her children with the little she has and still teaches them to stand tall.
She lives in the woman who tells her daughter,
'You are not here to suffer. You are here to conquer.

You are not small,
you are not weak,
you are not born to be crushed under someone else's feet.

You are Kali.
You are the storm they fear…'

A Single Hibiscus

I plucked it without ceremony,
one red hibiscus from *Appa's* garden.
Its petals, still warm from the sun,
creased slightly where my fingers held it too tight.

I placed it on a tray of fruits
Appa had chosen with care—
bright oranges, plump mangoes, bananas still green at the tips,
offerings with shape, with love.

No garland,
that's what stayed with me.
No garland for her neck,
where the skulls already hung like moons.

I stood in the crowd,
a stranger among her many children,
devotees shifting on their heels,
temple dogs curled in corners,
children tracing chalk lines with their toes.

And yet,
when the priest raised my single hibiscus
and pressed it to her chest,
nestled it among the jasmine,
something broke open.

That red, with the slightest hint of pink,
that colour against the white,

as if the world had stopped—
thamsagayahai.

She took it,
took it like it was everything,
like I had handed her
a secret I hadn't known I was keeping.

And then she spoke,
not with voice
but with that stillness
that floods the ears
when the world forgets to move.

It felt like a conversation
between two lovers
that only the two of us heard
and understood.

She said,
'You thought it was small.
You thought it wasn't enough.
But you came as you are.
And I,
I have always known the weight of that kind of offering.'

Around us, the temple moved on—
bells chimed, conches blew,
kids chased each other through incense clouds.
But I stood still,
anchored by her gaze,
by the fierce tenderness of being seen.

Later, I looked at the photo.
The frame held so little,
just a blur of flower, stone, and jasmine.
But I saw her.
I saw her saying yes.

And I knew
this was not worship.
This was recognition.
This was the goddess
meeting her beloved
in the hush between
heartbeat
and surrender.

Awakening

I have watched the rain,
the wings of the rain,
its abundance,
the vivid scarlet of its ferocious form.

I have watched the earth
weeping with the rain,
opening its arms to receive,
experiencing the rain's fiery passion of red.

Is the rain soothing the earth's yearning?
Is it yielding to the earth's longing?
Is it weeping, moved by the earth's love?

Who does the earth pine for?
Who does it miss fiercely?
The rain?
The clouds?
The sky?
Or is it simply parched for water?
Could both the earth and rain be relishing their roles?
For this is the universe's longing for itself?

V.
MYTH, BODY, AND BECOMING

(Rewriting myth, reclaiming the body,
women as witnesses, creators, and rebels)

Kali Does Not Wear White

These words came to me:

Irfan Khan
VidyaBalan
Elephants
Deep in the forest
Bitter gourd
Kabbadi
Big wok
Breasts
Margarita
AyushKejriwal
Five feet three
Kalakshetra
Mini Cooper
Durian
Raindrops on leaves
Vanilla- scented white candles

It works for me that we are co-creators
Naan Kadavul
Aham Brahmasmi

Kali does not sip margaritas.
She devours them, salt, lime, rim, and all,
then bites the glass into dust between her teeth.
She does not ask to be loved gently.
She wants the kind of love that shatters mirrors
and remembers past lives in bruises.

Irfan Khan once played a man who couldn't speak
but could stare with the eyes of a wounded panther.
Vidya Balan knew, her hips knew
what language lived in silence.
Kali speaks like that,
not with tongues but tides,
not with scripture but scars.

There are elephants deep in the forest
who carry the memory of temples in their bones.
They bow only to her,
the black-blooded mother
with a garland of heads
and a womb that smells of durian and war.

She cooks bitter gourd in a big wok,
stirring rage like spice,
a hunger older than the *Mahabharata*.

Ayush Kejriwal once stitched a sari
so blasphemously beautiful

it made even the gods bite their fists.
Kali wore it without a blouse,
breasts full and defiant
like galaxies.

She plays *kabbadi* with demons,
pulls them in, spits them out.
Kalakshetra never taught that choreography,
no *mudras* for revenge,
just a cracked fingernail
and a scream that breaks open
Mini Coopers in traffic.

She is five feet three
but taller than your lineage.
Your grandfather prayed to her.
Your mother fears her.
You light vanilla-scented candles
and call that peace.
She blows them out
and calls that beginning.

Raindrops on leaves sound like her laughter.
If you listen closely,
she is saying, '*Naan kadavul illai*—
I am not your God;
I am godlessness.
I am God becoming flesh,
then fire,
then nothing.

Aham Brahmasmi—
Look for the god within.'
And it works for me
that we are co-creators.
She paints my mouth with ash
and says,
'Go.
Un-name yourself.'

Twin Flame

You say I am your mother,
your mirror,
your omen.
You say I am the most beautiful woman
on earth,
and you say it like it's carved in stone,
not meant to be questioned,
not even by me.

Before every project
you pause.
What would she think?
What would she say?
My voice is your compass,
my eyes the firelight you must walk through
to know a thing is blessed.

You bring me your work
as if it were offerings at a shrine.
If I do not look, you wait.
You do not begin until I say,
'Go.'

You desire me in ways
that make the world disappear,
no room, no hour, no place too heavy
for the weight of our wanting.
When your hand touches mine,
I feel every woman

who was ever told to shrink
rise up inside me
and take her place.

We fight like gods in exile,
tearing down temples
only to rebuild them with our breath.
You walk away,
and the silence becomes unbearable.
Then you return,
as if the world never shifted,
and ask if I've eaten.

You let me leave, too.
You understand the storm in me
because it's the same one
you carry behind your ribs.
We rage and retreat
but always,
always circle back like moons,
where every footstep takes us back
to our shared gravity.

You study me,
not just my words
but the space between them.
You remember things I said once
quietly
in passing
and bring them back to me,
like rare stones
you never stopped carrying.

You do not love lightly.
You love with the full weight of your blood,
your silence,
your brilliance,
your flaws.

You call my chaos divine,
my mind an altar,
my presence a prophecy.
Who else has ever dared
to name me sacred?

You have said,
with a gaze that breaks me open,
that I am the sharpest mind
you have ever known,
that I am the love of your life,
that my rage is holy,
my silence pious,
my presence your resurrection.

You gave back to me
what I thought had died,
a self I buried in the wreckage
of what I had to survive.
You unearthed her
with nothing but devotion
and ruin
and fire.

And so, I call you what you are—
my twin flame,
my undoing,
my Kali.

Sanctum

'No. Not now,' she whispers,
not because she doesn't want to
but because she must first go home
and put her husband to bed
before sneaking back into the night to meet Lord Krishna.

Radha was never Krishna's wife.
Their love, sung by *bhajan* singers and temple bells,
was never sanctioned by law.
Dancers drape themselves in silk to mimic their passion,
but how many thought
they belonged to others, too?
That sacredness can arrive,
dressed in defiance?

You look at me
like you remember every inch of my body from another birth,
like you once built temples inside my ribcage
and burned incense in my throat.
Unconventional.
Unapologetic.
My lover, my whole world, wrapped in my mother's shawl.

Achammillai, achammillai, acham yenbathillaiye—
No fear… no fear.
Is that chorus only for activists,
those waving flags in protest?

Or can it be for us too,
two people courageous enough
to choose desire over obedience?

Your chest welded to mine,
our skin, borderless,
our breath, one long refusal.

Cymbals clash,
drums pound like our pulse,
incense and myrrh spiral through the temple's air,
priests chant,
but none of them can summon God
like the way your mouth finds mine.

You come for me like the morning breeze,
soft but unstoppable.
You find me in the space that is ours,
hidden, carved by need and memory.
My heart lurches
not from fear
but from the sheer ache of being seen.

At the entrance to our sanctuary,
everything stops,
except the rustle of silk against my hips
and the heat of your hands
pressing me into you.

We are not sinners in the dark corner of the temple.
We are scripture,
we are prayer,

we are the sanctity they fear,
delirious, wet, breathless,
meditative, silent, knowing.

The gods in their polished grandeur,
decked in gold, stiff in poise,
pale next to us.
We, tangled and naked,
are more divine than stone,
drenched in sweat and something holier.

And she watches us,
the goddess with tangled hair
and red smile split wide,
Kali, bare and blinding,
not modest, not moral,
a body clothed in cosmos.
Her laughter cracks the sky.

Is this love a sin
just because it doesn't kneel before convention?
Is it criminal to be held by a man
like I am made of stars and storm?
Must we always pretend
that union is only sacred
when a priest says so?

She dances,
not for them but for us.
Skulls clink at her neck.
Her breasts shake like thunderclouds.
And we,

we tremble, not from shame
but from awe.

This is not fiction.
This is not metaphor.
This is memory.

Kali showed us her truest form,
unmasked, unbound,
with teeth bared
and thighs parted.
And in that moment,
she shattered every chain.

Perhaps this is why we found each other again, here
in this lifetime where love dares to sweat,
where nothing needs to be hidden,
where your touch is a ritual,
where my moan is holy,
where guilt is a ghost we no longer feed.

Where I, with you,
am not less than sacred
but more.

Why Look for Kali Elsewhere?

You journeyed through the world
as if it were made of glass,
never breaking anything
yet leaving behind
a new shape in the air.

There was nothing loud
about your grace.
It moved like rose water,
unseen yet unforgettable,
marking everything
it touched.

You knew which parts of yourself
to make visible
and which to fold into a sari pleat,
bordered in silence and poise.
You were not draped
but enthroned.
Humility was your crown.

You never spoke of sophistication
as though it belonged to others.
It was in your hands,
in how you sliced mangoes,
in the way you wrapped pain
into sweet rice for guests.
You knew exactly

how much salt to add
to someone's sorrow.

You didn't need temples;
you made offerings
with turmeric fingers,
chanted while chopping greens,
saw omens in spilled rice
and stray crows.

What others called gentleness
was the quiet edge of your fury.
You held the world
like a new born,
but no one dared
steal from your arms.

Your love for me
was not poetic;
it was survival,
the kind that stood
between me and the world,
hands bare, eyes unflinching.
You loved me with a fierceness
I have since mistaken
for gods and thunder.
Now I know
your love did not roar;
it stood still and burned.

When you scolded,
the earth steadied itself.

When you laughed,
I forgot what I was afraid of.
You were the first one
to make my name sound sacred.
No one says, 'Have you eaten?' the same.

Why should I go looking for Kali
in any temple
when your voice,
sharp, sacred,
summoned the storm
and gave me breath?

You sang
with that tiny book in hand,
thin pages inked
with the ache of poets
and the joy of movies.
You never missed a word
and gave cinema its soul.

After you left,
festivals forgot how to arrive.
Pongal boiled over with less meaning,
Diwali lamps flickered
like they were waiting
for you to light them right.

The house now feels
like a prayer
said without intention.

Every room echoes
the note of your absence.

And the air tastes
like something's missing.
I look for you
in jasmine strands,
in the smell of sandalwood,
in the sudden stillness before rain.
And I find you
in bitter gourd,
in neem leaves,
in the pause between questions.

You were my first temple,
red-eyed and beautiful,
graceful even in rage.
Amma, why would I look for Kali in stone
when you lived and died as her?

Letter to My Father

He never held me like something fragile.
He let me fall, bruise, break.
He stood over the wreckage and said, 'Good. Now you know
what hurts and what doesn't.'

When the police told me I could be arrested if I didn't bend,
he didn't tell me to be careful.
He said, 'If you are arrested for doing your job,
I will be the proudest father on earth.'
And I believed him.
I still do.

My father,
spine straight as memory,
heart quiet as a monsoon sky
just before it breaks,
moves through the world
as if it were sacred and wounded.

He once told me:
'When you give, be very grateful to the person who is
receiving,
for without him, you have lost an opportunity to serve.
And when you give, make sure the person receiving does not
feel humiliated.'
These words are my *Bhagavad Gita.*
They live in my marrow.

He taught me
that dignity is not worn like a crown
but carried like water,
balanced,
fluid,
life-giving.

Appa,
never loud in his goodness,
never needing applause.
He does not know
how in his eyes
I see Kali grinning,
blood on her tongue,
flowers in her hair,
how in his hands
I see her power made tender,
made holy,
made real.

Appa,
you are my beginning,
my becoming.
You have taught me
that even the fiercest gods
kneel sometimes
to touch the earth
with love.

Letter to My Son

You were born in the shadow of whispers,
conceived before rings, before blessings, before anyone could call it decent.
I carried you like contraband,
married your father without my parents' eyes on me.
The ceremony was holy;
the aftermath was mine to bear.

And yet, your first years were nothing but sunlight.
You lived in my parents' house,
their hands soft around you,
their laughter spilling over your crib.
In those days, Kali sat in the corner of the room,
her sword resting flat across her lap,
watching you with an expression I couldn't read.
You were adored so completely
that I almost forgot she was there.

But the day came when you saw me walk back into another kind of home,
one where doors slammed like gunshots,
where the air went still before the storm of his voice,
where I learned again to shrink my body
to make myself a smaller target.
You learned it, too.
The boy who had once been praised for every word
began to speak less and less.

School slipped away from you.
Homework went untouched.
Your eyes drifted somewhere beyond the room,
and no teacher could follow you there.
They saw a boy who couldn't focus.
They didn't see the way you were tracking every mood,
every shift in my tone,
every danger in the house we couldn't leave.
Kali had risen from her seat,
her anklets ringing softly,
but she wasn't here for me.
She stood inside you,
her breath warming your spine,
and I feared the day she would draw her sword.

And then one day, she did,
not in violence but in defiance.
She burned through the fog around you,
split it clean with her blade,
and you walked out into the open.
It was the day you became older than me.

From there, you didn't walk, you surged:
Two Dean's Lists,
Bachelor's,
Master's.
And still, when I look at you,
I see the boy once curled in a corner.
Only now, Kali stands beside him,
ankles in the mud,
mouth blood-red with victory,

her hand resting lightly on his shoulder.
Prathee,
you are my joy and my reckoning,
my ruin and my resurrection,
the proof that what's broken can still tower over its ruins,
the proof that a child loved fiercely
will always find his way back to himself.

So walk, my son,
with your feet in the mud,
with your teeth red from the fight,
with Kali's sword in your hands,
and never again lower your head for anyone.

Letter to My Other Mother

You don't believe in God,
and yet, there you are,
louder than scripture,
more fearless than fire,
and warmer than the sun on a bruised back.

You don't do reverence.
You scoff at incense and side-eye rituals.
You wear your rage like bangles—loud, clinking.
You don't bow your head.
You tilt your chin up,
like you're daring the world to try you.

You're not my birth mother,
and yet, you are Gowrie.
You hold space the way temples should,
wide, weathered, and always open.

Since Gowrie left,
since her body curled into silence,
it's been your voice
that has carried me back to myself.

You don't see it,
but I watch you with the eyes of the girl I used to be,
the one afraid to take up space.
You kicked doors open with your opinions.
You made me tea and revolution in the same breath.
You raised your middle finger at the polite rot of diplomacy

and taught me that kindness isn't passive;
it's a fucking roar.

You are my Kali,
not the blood-drenched one of myth
but the one who calls me 'daft cow'
and then makes sure I've eaten,
the one who stands for justice
like it's stitched into her DNA
and doesn't care if her voice
makes men flinch.

You've never asked to be worshipped.
That's what makes you divine.
You've never tried to be anyone's God.
That's what makes you holy.

And maybe you'll never believe it,
but I see you, Shavi,
barefoot in the middle of the riot,
one hand holding me steady,
the other flipping the bird at the sky.

I don't need altars;
I just need you
exactly as you are—
unapologetic, unbowed, unmistakably mine.

VI.
RUPTURE, EARTH, AND RETURN

(Earth, mortality, resolution, peace-making, and the voice reborn)

The Flow of the Earth

My love, my Kali
Could we stand naked in the sun,
absorb its light into our being,
and vanish to the eye of others
so as to remain united forever on this earth,
to become nothing and one at the same time?

Ganapathy's Balloon

It's the nose they mocked first,
elongated, flat,
a remnant of the cursed crash,
metal, bone, and flame.

And then the ears, too wide for his face,
and the belly, rounded,
like the Hindu god with the elephant head.

They called him Lord Ganapathy
not out of reverence
but ridicule;
later, just LG,
like the TV,
broadcasting nothing
but loneliness in HD.
He has worn the nickname
like a blister for decades.

For twenty years, he has endured
taunts like daily *prasad.*
Now, at twenty-four,
he wears silk shirts and mirrored shades,
strutting like a peacock on hot concrete,
chest puffed, voice crude,
catcalling girls and aunties,
who cross the street when they see him coming.

Because behind the swagger
is a secret blooming
into monstrous shape—
horniness, swollen and wild,
has taken form.
Not a thought,
not a desire
but a thing.

A balloon,
stretching out of his body
and above the roof of his three-storey house,
shaped like an elephant's trunk
but made of nothing found in nature,
a pulsating mix of brown, orange, green, and pink,
like lust fermenting with shame.

No one can see it….yet,
except him.
It glows in the dark,
a long, twisting, neon banner
of unmet need
and buried fear.

He kneels to Ganesha, to Vishnu, to Muruga.
He chants, pleads,
hopes the villagers don't look up at night
and see the thing
arcing above his home like a signpost of failure.

He's terrified
because once they see the glow,

they'll know:
LG is not a man who gets women.
He is just a man who wants
and fails.

And when the first girl giggles,
pointing to the streak of pink light
faintly glistening above the mango tree,
he knows the laughter has begun.

That's when
Kali comes.

Not in silk, not with pity
but bare-breasted,
eyes blazing,
tongue lolling in rage and laughter.

She does not ask for permission.
She arrives like lightning,
necklace of skulls jangling
to the beat of his humiliation.

She sees the balloon.
She laughs…not cruel
but ancient,
a mother who's watched too many sons
inflate their shame into a spectacle.

'Oh, little god of broken men!'
she hisses.
'Look at the temple you've built

for your hunger.
Is this your prayer,
a neon cock on the roof of your longing?'

She doesn't touch it.
She touches him,
his heart trembling,
his skin cold,
his pride brittle.

And for the first time,
Ganapathy weeps
not for what he wants
but for what he's become.

The balloon flickers,
sags,
not gone
but grounded,
small enough
to carry.

In the morning,
he walks the street,
shirt unbuttoned,
no shades,
no smirk,
just a man
with a shadow the size of his truth.

And the girls don't laugh.
They stare,

then look away.
The night sky stays dark,
and for once,
so does the roof.

Kali & I are One and the Same

Well-oiled braids,
a black *pottu* in between my eyebrows, gold ornaments,
the soft rustle of silk, and
the family honour etched in my vagina.

'Good girls don't run along corridors.'
The nun's glare silences my voice in the convent.

'Don't bring us shame,'
words from relatives stuck on the walls at home.

And then came menstrual blood.

Theeddu they warn.
'Dirty? Why am I dirty?'
The mirror reflects a single plait, red *bindi*, curves hidden
carefully under yards of cloth…and a lost childhood.

Chants, clanging of bells, Kali in my parents' altar,
black complexioned,
skulls in place of jewellery,

heavy breasts enticing,
matted hair unrestrained,
tongue protruding...

My father falls at Kali's feet.
So do the powerful and powerless,
but when would they question her lack of modesty?

What if I, too, dance freely,
the brown of my skin shimmering,
the wind snuggling into my heaving tits,
the sun wearing itself as my crown,
the rain kissing the ground to the rhythm of my anklets, wild
curly hair swinging furiously,
skeletons enhancing my nudity,
arms forming gestures on the clouds,
feet caressing the womb of Mother Earth?

Would I then become Kali,
the mother, the seductress, the lover,
the unconditional love and compassion,
the destroyer of the dark...?

And would you then come beyond the whirlpool of
ignorance and dance with me?
For I am the eye of the storm...

Waging Peace in a World of Conflict

It is not the absence of sound
but the quiet hum beneath the scream,
the stillness that cuts through the wound,
and where our broken self finds the shore.

It is neither the end of war
nor the silence after the gun
but the courage to stand up straight
despite being kicked to the ground,
to see through the intoxication of manoeuvres,
of what divides, and still be one.

It is the hand that reaches across,
the lines we draw, the fences we build.
It is the might of the heart
that crushes the divisive narrative.

It is the child who dreams in the dark,
while bombs fall, deafening as thunder,
the spark, the smallest of light
that whispers, 'Begin again and again and again….'

Peace is not just the soil where hatred dies
but the seed that dares to grow,
the truth that strips away the deception,
and the strength to let it show.

It is neither a place nor a distant star
but the space between the chaos and the calm,

between the birth and final breath,
between the wound and healing balm,
between the living and death.

In the stillness of the night, where shadows dance,
she emerges, dark, naked, ferocious,
her tongue a crimson flame, her eyes a trance.
They call her fierce, her form a menace,
A tempest of fury, a force untamed.
But in her wrath, peace blooms,
like white flowers in a vast field.

They name her chaos and shiver at her wrath,
a storm that tears the world apart.
But peace is not the loud absence
of war, of pain, of human cries
but the courage to raise your middle finger at power
for the broken bodies, severed limbs covered in political lies.

Her necklace of skulls, a garland in place of gold,
each one a story, a battle, a cry.
Her sword, a stroke of blinding truth,
cuts through the masks the powerful wear,
revealing their end is furiously near,
death, the permanence that's always there.

She dances on the edge of sense,
where borders blur and flags decay,
her steps, a rhythm so intense
it births new worlds, where walls are swept away.

For Kali does not come to merely destroy

but to strip away the trumped-up fibs,
for the story untold,
for the birthing of voices that rise strong,
the song that rights your ancient wrong!

Like Kali, peace is neither a gentle stream
nor the eternal resting of the soul
but the infinite, the boundless dream.
Would you dare to envision it with me?

The World is Thirsty, So Write

Have you truly watched water, knelt by its origins, where it springs new born from the earth's dark womb, where it laughs over pebbles like a child remembering her first secret?

Have you observed the river's silent communion with stone—no conflict, only cosmic choreography where its water glides over obstructions like a monk's fingers over prayer beads, each ripple a sacred syllable in liquid Sanskrit? It carries the primordial knowing that even the most adamant resistance will, through the patient stroke of centuries, become smooth as a moonstone altar. Have you ever understood this is not mere movement but the universe's slow exhalation where the polished curves of stones become scriptures?

Have you seen the water's fury when the river becomes a clenched fist, hurling the sky's reflection back at the heavens? The same currents that cradled the clouds now wear their drowned faces as jewellery.

To watch water is to see the world twice: once as it is, once as it could be. Just like a woman is: gentle warmth and unbridled force. Just as Kali is: the dutiful consort of the ultimate cosmic Shiva, or the celestial badass!

Like rain, seductive as a whisper one moment and a roaring force the next, peace is what grows in the wake of a storm. It can be the hush between heartbeats or the courage after shattered worlds rearrange themselves.

Yes, peace was once a battleground. But writers do not flinch. They write it dirty, write it real, for the page is not a sanctuary; it's a space where they plant verbs like land mines, where metaphors bloom through cracks in the concrete of reality. Then they shape the words that come after: the remembering, the mending, the slow unfurling of the new. Even though writing is no delicate work, even if hands shake with the aftershocks of war, their pen stitch sentences while sirens wail like mothers whose sons were butchered.

They write not to smooth over wounds but to make the scars speak in languages so visceral even storm clouds halt their thunder to listen. Every sentence becomes a threshold, holding both the wreckage and the rebuilding, the raw scream and the lullaby that follows. This is how ink becomes alchemy: spinning pain into bridges, weaving absence into a loom where new narratives might grow, just like the work of rivers carving canyons, of roots breaking rocks.

Like water, writers obey no *fatwa* but their own relentless truth. They let their words erode walls, travel across the surface of minds, rippling outwards, for a story can be the flood that drowns hatred, leaving behind fertile ground.

Still, water is the bravest mirror. It shows the sky's tantrums and the tree's amputated limbs without apology. Writers are equally merciless in their clarity, for healing built on sanitised history is rot dressed as roses. Only then their page upon page becomes a pool where readers see their own fractures, their own wars, and perhaps, their possibilities.

And when the world erupts in fire, writers, like water, refuse extinction. They become the mist that slips through barbed wires, the glacier that patiently grinds mountains to sand, the tidal surge that swallows the shorelines of complacency. Their words rise like vapour, freeze into bridges, surge like a tide. Their stories pull us back towards each other, even if written behind cages.

Peace is a living water, relentless, adaptable, and infinitely patient.

And in its endless flow, we will keep finding the only truth that matters: nothing is so broken that it can't be transformed.

ABOUT THE AUTHOR

Mahi Ramakrishnan is a poet/writer, documentary filmmaker, and forced-migration consultant/researcher whose work lives at the sharp edges of women's power, political resistance, and the untidy truths of survival. A former journalist, she has worked with international outlets including *Time* magazine, the BBC, the Associated Press, and Agence France-Presse, grounding her creative practice in years of rigorous reporting from the field. She is also the current president of PEN Malaysia.

Her storytelling is shaped by long-term work alongside displaced communities, survivors of conflict-related sexual violence, and grassroots refugee women's groups that anchor her life and politics. Moving between documentation and imagination, her work refuses the distance of neutrality, choosing instead to bear witness from within.

Mahi's poetry moves like a blade; cutting through silence, memory, and the polite violence of the world. She writes from the crossroads of activism and ritual, where myth bleeds into lived experience and the feminine divine refuses to stay tame. In these poems, Mahi reimagines Kali as political, feral, tender, and unbound: an echo of Gowrie, the woman who birthed and raised her and the countless others still fighting to be seen.

This is her debut poetry collection.

during Dasain.

Pokhari——— Water tank, pond.

Prabasi——— Countryman domiciled out of the country.

Pradhan——— Head (man) of a group.

Pudke——— Shorty.

Pujas, Pooja——— Worship.

Purnima——— Full moon.

Pyari———Darling, beloved.

R. Rahdahni———'Right of Way', travelling permit.

Rakchesh———Demon.

Raksha Dal———Defence forces.

Rakshi——— Locally brewed drink.

Rani——— Queen, consort.

Rickshawallah———Person who pulls or pedals a rickshaw.

Rupee——— Denomination of money.

S. Saab———Short for Sahib, Sir.

Sagarmatha——— Nepalese name of Mt. Everest.

Sarkar——— Most revered Sir, Excellency.

Sallaghari———Pine grove, pine trees in a group.

Sange Chom Khemde—I fall at the feet of the Lord.

Saptah——— Seven day ceremony of recitation of the Scriptures.

Saris——— Cloth wrapped around body as apparel by women.

Sarong———Lungi, a type of apparel worn by both men and women.

Sathi——— Friend.

Sena———Force of fighting personnel.

Shreepech———Headgear.

Stupa———Large hemispherical structure surmounted by the all seeing eyes of the Buddha. A place of worship.

Glossary 6

T. Ta — Tamang word for horse.

Tamang — One of the tribes of Nepal, the word itself meaning a trader of horses.

Thadodando — Steep hill.

Tika — Placing of the mark of any colour, particularly red, on the forehead.

Tole — Quarter of a town.

Tundikhel — Parade ground at Kathmandu.

Tihar — The annual festival which comes about three weeks after Dasain, called also Diwali, Festival of Lights, and Bhai Tika (Brother's Day).

Glossary 4

Magne—— Beg, ask for.

Maharaj——Old term for Rana Prime Minister.

Maharajdhiraj—— King.

Mahdal—— Drum like instrument which one plays with hands.

Mahila—— Second son.

Manakamana—— Wish come true.

Mang—— Tamang word for trader in horses.

Mani—— Memorial to dead relatives. (Buddhist).

Marbari, marwari——Busines traders of Rajasthan stock but now settled and conducting business elsewhere.

Mukti—— Liberation.

Mulmi—— Village or clan headman.

N. Navah—— Nine day cermony of recitation of Scriptures.

Nwaran——Name giving ceremony of newborn.

P. Paley—— Watchman.

Paltans——Military company.

Panchas—— Village representatives, elders.

Pancha Baja—— Musical instruments played by Damais.

Pandit—— Priest.

Pashmina——Pure soft wool used for making shawls.

Paso——Trap, snare.

Patuka——Long strip of cloth wrapped round the waist.

Peepal——A type of tree of the fig family, considered sacred in Nepal.

Phulpati—— Ceremony of bringing flowers home

		inscribed on stone tablets and kept in a circumscribed area.
	Hunchha	Yes.
J.	Jai	Honour to, victory to.
	Jai Durga Mata	Honour to Mother Durga.
	Jamadar	Military rank.
	Jamara	Barley plants grown at Dasain in the Dasain room.
	Jat	Caste.
	Jhankri	Shaman, witch doctor.
	Jhyaali	News announcement by beat of drums.
K.	Kaley	Blackie.
	Khardar	Civil rank.
	Khari ko bot	A tree in the midst of the Tundikhel where the Rana rulers used to collect on special occasions. Now no longer there.
	Khukri	Traditional knife of the Gurkhas.
	Kila	Boundary pillar.
	Kirpan	Miniature dagger of the Sikhs, a race in India.
	Kirya	Twelve days of observance for the death of a kinsman.
	Kitapi	Book-keeper, especially registration of appointments.
	Ko	Of.
	Kurnesh	Form of greeting of seniors.
L.	Lahure, Lahure dai	Recruit or personnel in military service.
	Lama	Buddhist priest.
	Lungi	Sarong, traditional dress.
M.	Ma, Mata	Form of address for mother,

	Bur	A type of tree.
	Burja	Gables of a house, a tower.
C.	Chaityas	Miniature stupas.
	Chameli	Jasmine.
	Chang	Fermented rice drink.
	Chyakhura	Type of partridge.
D.	Dai	Elder brother.
	Dal	Military camping platoon.
	Damai	Tailors cum ministrels.
	Darshan	Sight audience of Seniors.
	Dasain, Dashahara	Major festival of puja to Durga.
	Dashami	Tenth day of lunar month.
	Deurali	Hill top.
	Dharmaputra	Adopted son.
	Dharmasala	Caravanserai.
	Dhungri	Ear ring.
	Doko	Wicker basket.
	Dui	Two.
	Durbar	Palace.
	Durga	A goddess.
F.	Farka	Return. (Imperative)
	Felty	Fatigue cap.
G.	Gaucharan	Pasture land.
	Ghyang	Buddhist temple.
	Gurkhas	Generally applied to Nepalese in any army.
	Gorkhali	Term used as synonym of Nepali.
	Guruju	Preceptor, member of Guruju family also.
H.	Hakim	Boss.
	Havaldar	Military rank.
	Hiki	Prayers and names of Gods

GLOSSARY

To create an an atmosphere of Nepalese and Burmese environment, words in both languages have been included in the narrative; and, with a view to maintain without interruption the course of the reader's progress, meanings of some of these words have also been provided within brackets. In order, however to include all such words together for easier reference, all such words and their meanings are given in the index. Burmese words in the text are printed in italics.

NEPALESE TERMS

A. Aitabar—————— Sunday.

Arghan—————— Funeral rites on the forty–fifth day of death.

Armywallah————— Fellow, Man in the army.

Athpariya————— Whole day aide (de Camp).

B. Ba———————Father.

Bada———————Big.

Bahadur—————— Brave, also used as middle name in names of certain classes and castes.

Bahun, Brahmin—— Priestly class.

Beli———————— A creeper – jasmine like.

Bhailo——————— Money collection during Tihar festival in the same way as 'waits' in England.

Bhaitika—————— Brother's Day during Tihar festival.

Bir———————— Brave, also used as a name.

Bot———————— Tree.

Bulakis—— ——— Nose ring, worn through the septum.